I0186632

Camouflage
Of
Perfection

Lenita Cornett

BK
ROYSTON
Publishing

BK Royston Publishing
P. O. Box 4321
Jeffersonville, IN 47131
502-802-5385
http://www.bkroystonpublishing.com
bkroystonpublishing@gmail.com

© Copyright – 2017

All Rights Reserved. No part of this book
may be reproduced, stored in a retrieval
system, or transmitted by any means without
the written permission of the author.

Cover Design: Greater Works Designs
@info@greaterworksds.com

ISBN-13:978-1-946111-28-9
ISBN-10:1-946111-28-7

Printed in the United States of America

Dedication

I would like to dedicate my work to my husband, Floyd Lynn Cornett, Jr. for being my rock.

I would like to dedicate my work to Stacey Pritchett, no matter near or far she still manages to be there for me.

I would also like to dedicate my work to three powerful women that were part of my circle in my time of need.

They are now my Sisters for Life:

Latize Daniel

Trenise Welch

Valinda Lewis

Table of Contents

Introduction

Camouflaged Perfectionism

Who has ever had the feeling of not wanting to get out of bed to go to work? You just want to sleep and rest. You emotionally eat comfort food that you know is not healthy, but it makes you feel good for the moment. Well, those were my feelings. Nothing could be right enough, so I would spend countless hours spinning my wheels on preparing for just about everything. That is just one aspect, but I will go further as you keep reading. Let me go back to the feelings mentioned. Lack of energy, motivation, healthy eating, burnout, self-deception and feeling like you are 'not good enough' are all feelings that impact our psyche, no matter who you are regardless of social or ethnic background. The list of feelings mentioned, were my watchwords. How did I get to this point? I am glad you asked. It all goes back to being my worst critic, comparing my success to others, and allowing other individual's opinion of me to validate who I was as a person and leader. Let's wind the clock back over two years to take you on my journey.

Camouflage

Of

Perfection

"Company, Attention"

As a senior leader, I was blessed to be appointed to serve as a First Sergeant for my organization. It was the most rewarding and best position I had ever done while serving as a leader. My daily hours of work during the week averaged 15 hours, and the weekends averaged 5 hours due to me preparing my schedule to be ready for the following week. Now add 15 hours for 5 days and 5 hours for the weekend. My mind and body would remind me that I couldn't handle the overload. So, my body would shut down at least two hours after I got home from work. Floyd would remind me that I was working too hard. I felt bad when I took time off on my weekends when it was actually time off. I did not have a great social life after work or on weekends. This is just a quick synopsis of my workload to give you an idea of how many hours I worked.

Not to mention, I still had to get up to conduct my leaders huddle meeting before my company did our daily physical training. So can you imagine how my body was feeling? There were several days that I was not effective in my mind, body, and soul, all

1

because I did not get enough rest. Even when I slept, my mind was racing with what I needed to for the next day. So as I share with you a quick glimpse of my story, there are a few things to learn. In order to give your best and to be your best, you must identify the areas that are keeping you stuck. Those emotions are the barriers that need to be identified, so you can have the self- discovery of what is needed to help make you better. You can't help anyone if you can't help yourself.

Tip: Identify the behaviors of perfection and how it impacts your overall well-being.

_____

_____

_____

_____

_____

_____

_____

_____

_____

_____

_____

_____

_____

_____

_____

_____

_____

_____

_____

_____

_____

_____

_____

_____

"Forward, March"

All of the emotions that I described earlier didn't happen overnight. They built up from years of constantly battling to be better at challenging myself. Don't get me wrong, I am not saying that it is not important to constantly look at areas in your life to challenge and improve you. I am simply saying that when you are constantly working to be better and challenging yourself, you don't treat that moment as priority and you as the last priority. That is what I did; it didn't make it right, but it happened. I worked so hard for the next challenge; the next position, and the next promotion. Do you see the trend? All the while, doubting my leadership abilities because of others success and because of what someone else thought of me. Working long hours to be 'proactive' and not 'reactive' but was still not effective because of the burnout feeling. I was eating fast food every day, because I was too tired to take the time to actually cook a healthy meal. Actually Floyd has always done the cooking, so I would not get home at a good time to eat a healthy meal before 7 P.M.

All of this goes back to me feeling like I was not good enough. I tried so hard to not make mistakes, in which I made plenty. I was afraid of failure. I asked the question to God, "Why did this happen to me?" I had to get help, or I was going to either collapse from burnout or have a severe case of anxiety and depression. I had to request through my medical provider to see a therapist for anxiety and stress. I also shared my emotions with close friends that supported me. I surrounded myself with positive people. I prayed and meditated. I had to trust and lean on my Team regardless of the "naysayers" and their opinions. All of these actions that I mentioned helped me improve my overall well-being spiritually, emotionally, physically, and socially. I am going to leave this quote with you from a good friend that resonates with me today.

"Be strong enough to stand alone, smart enough to know when you need help, and brave enough to ask for it"-Duke Smith

Tip: Take the time to find ways to embrace your imperfections to improve your overall well-being.

_____
_____
_____
_____
_____
_____
_____
_____
_____
_____
_____
_____
_____
_____
_____
_____
_____
_____
_____
_____
_____
_____

"Company, Halt"

So I just spoke about the different actions that I took to help my overall well-being. Now that I've gained the tools that equipped me, I still had to move forward and face other obstacles. I still had to deal with individuals that spoke negatively about me, but didn't know me. So remember, I spoke earlier about doubting my abilities because of others opinion of me. Anytime I would start to think a negative thought, I had to remind myself of what I went through and what God had pushed me through. Everything that happened to me was not a mistake. It happened to build my strength and confidence. I am not ashamed that I had to seek help for anxiety and stress. Where would I be if I didn't ask for someone's hand? I share this with you to emphasize the importance of 'YOU'. Sometimes you just have to stop where you are, breath, regroup and get your mind back to a positive state of mind.

.

Tip: Even through your daily obstacles, take a pause and breath

_____

_____

_____

_____

_____

_____

_____

_____

_____

_____

_____

_____

_____

_____

_____

_____

_____

_____

_____

_____

_____

"Parade, Rest"

With all the tips that were mentioned, you are now on your way to self-reflection and improvement. Self-reflection is time for self-assessment, which in turn helps with improving your behaviors that will create the best you inside and out. The more you practice, the more you will notice that your mind will reach a state of calmness, peace, and clarity. This takes time, but the more you are focused on creating positive change, the more you will realize that your imperfections help you build strength and confidence to tackle any challenge that comes your way.

Say these words of affirmation with me.

'I am more than enough.'

'My life's obstacles are a pathway to my success and destiny.'

'I am a light in the world's darkest place.'

'I am here as an example of healing and strength.'

'My scars are my beauty.'

'Perfection is not reality, but my imperfections are the pieces of me that I love and accept.'

"Perfection is achieved, not when there is nothing more to add, but when there is nothing left to take away"
Antoine de Saint-Exupery

'I am more than enough.'

_____
_____
_____
_____
_____
_____
_____
_____
_____
_____
_____
_____
_____
_____
_____
_____
_____
_____
_____
_____
_____
_____

'My life's obstacles are a pathway to my success and destiny.'

_____
_____
_____
_____
_____
_____
_____
_____
_____
_____
_____
_____
_____
_____
_____
_____
_____
_____
_____
_____
_____

'I am a light in the world's darkest place.'

'I am here as an example of healing and strength.'

_____

_____

_____

_____

_____

_____

_____

_____

_____

_____

_____

_____

_____

_____

_____

_____

_____

_____

_____

_____

_____

'My scars are my beauty.'

_____

_____

_____

_____

_____

_____

_____

_____

_____

_____

_____

_____

_____

_____

_____

_____

_____

_____

_____

_____

_____

_____

'Perfection is not reality, but my imperfections are the pieces of me that I love and accept.'

———————————————————
———————————————————
———————————————————
———————————————————
———————————————————
———————————————————
———————————————————
———————————————————
———————————————————
———————————————————
———————————————————
———————————————————
———————————————————
———————————————————
———————————————————
———————————————————
———————————————————
———————————————————
———————————————————
———————————————————

Lenita F. Cornett, B.S., DSL, LSSBB(C)

Lenita Cornett is the Visionary and Founder of Purple Camouflaged Mentor LLC and She is Perfectly Made Community. She is a mentor, author, life and transformational strategist/coach who is passionate about connecting, networking and helping women overcome the struggles of perfectionism.

Lenita continues to proudly service in the U.S. Army with 21 years of service as a senior leader. She is currently stationed at Fort McCoy, Wisconsin where she serves an Observer Coach and Trainer for Reserve and National Guard units. She earned her Bachelor's degree in Business Administration with concentration of Human Resources. She is a certified Demonstrated Senior Logistician, Lean Six Sigma Black Belt Candidate, Master Resiliency Trainer, and Life Coach.

Lenita started her journey after successfully completing her tenure as First Sergeant in the U.S. Army. After experiencing many lessons learned with her own struggles of perfectionism and the negative impacts, she was inspired to empower women and share her story that through faith and perseverance she is a recovering perfectionist. She is Perfectly Made Community was created to provide a community for women of active duty, veterans of the Armed Forces, civil service and all who support her efforts to empower, educate, uplift, inspire, develop and thrive while winning the battle of perfectionism with confidence.

Lenita has been featured in radio interviews with Camouflaged Sisters LLC and the Veteran Women LLC. She is married to her husband Floyd Lynn Cornett, Jr of 16 years.

Awards
National Association of Professional Women as its VIP Woman of the Year Circle, 2014-2015

Author Camouflaged Sisters: Revealing the Struggles of the Black Woman's Military Experience, 2015

The Camouflage of Perfection, 2017

Reach out to Lenita Cornett on Social Media

Facebook: Lenita Cornett
https://www.facebook.com/lenita.cornett

Facebook Group: She is Perfectly Made
Community
https://www.facebook.com/groups/sheisperf
ectlymade/

Twitter: Lenita Cornett
https://twitter.com/lenitacornett

Instagram:
http://www.instagram.com/lenitaspeaks

Website:
http://www.sheisperfectlymade.com

www.ingramcontent.com/pod-product-compliance
Lightning Source LLC
Chambersburg PA
CBHW051714090426
42736CB00013B/2701